Spiritual Gifts In The 21st Century

By
Dr. Stephen Zemanek

2

978-1-387-09648-0

Dedication

This book is dedicated to the men and women who serve faithfully on staff at Set Free Mission Bible Training Center in Greenville, KY. Set Free focuses on restoring men and women who've lost everything due to addictions. Their faithful work provides a place where people can learn to live free of addiction through a meaningful relationship with Jesus Christ.

Other Books by Dr. Stephen Zemanek include:
1. Discovering Satisfaction In Life, A Study of Ecclesiastes
(Leader's/Student's Guides)
2. Become the Teacher Students Love to Hear
3. Seeing God Monday Through Saturday
6. Zephaniah The Day of the Lord (Leader's/Student Guides)
7. Taking Jesus To Court
8. Ask The Pastor
9. Revelation: A Group Study Guide (Teacher/Student Editions)
10. What Makes A Great Bible Teacher?
11. Build A Life Worth Living
12. Proverbs in Real Life
13. Lessons in Joy
14. Deliberately Simple Thoughts on Life
15. Jesus is Enough
16. Regret-Free Living
17. Prayers That Changes Everything!
18. If God Heals, Why Am I Still Sick?
19. Build a Life Worth Living
20. What's So Great About Jesus?
21. Living The Satisfied Life
22. The Uncharted Journey
23. Daniel: God Is Still In Control

Contents

Introduction

It was a warm Northern California evening. I was seated on the front row waiting to preach as a guest. The church was full and the lead minister asked for those who needed healing to come forward for prayer. As the music played and the congregation worshiped key leaders began praying for those who had come forward for help. What caught my attention over the sound of music, singing, and prayer were the words "You just don't have enough faith to be healed." The recipient of this horrible statement was a young lady - now in tears - trying to convince the person praying for her that she did trust God. After a brief and unfriendly rebuke the person praying sent her back to her seat with the words "God heals everyone who has enough faith. I prayed for you and you didn't receive healing so you must not have enough faith."

I sat there heartbroken and stunned because of the callousness of this leader toward someone who was so desperately in need. I was still trying to come to grips with what I'd witnessed as they introduced me and I took the platform to speak. Following the service I spoke with the lead minister at the church to share my concerns over what happened during the time of prayer. Without hesitation he informed me that everything said to this lady was proper and in line with scripture. After much discussion we both left unconvinced by the other's argument. This would be a sad story if it were a unique aberration. It is a tragic story because it illustrates one of many common misunderstandings about spiritual gifts within the church.

I've spent the majority of my adult life ministering in the Pentecostal and Charismatic portion of the church.

Over the years I have seen incredible moves of the Holy Spirit which have taken my breath away. I have also seen equally bizarre moves of emotion and ego which have made me question the reality of the gifts all together. Without offering any specific details I can say that I have witnessed people screaming during church services and others convulsing while claiming to be under the Holy Spirit's direction. With acts like this is it any wonder some people shy away from the topic of spiritual gifts?

Compounding the confusion over the gifts of the Holy Spirit are all the respected voices on this subject sharing different opinions. On the topic of spiritual gifts within the 21st century church, godly leaders offer very different opinions. Some teach gifts of the Holy Spirit like healing no longer exist and others teach anyone pretending to move in a gift of the Holy Spirit is either emotionally unstable or demon possessed. However, other teachers who are equally well educated teach that the gifts of the Holy Spirit are in operation within the 21st century church. They go on to offer ample evidence and examples from congregations around the world. With such a divergent opinion on the topic is it any wonder many choose to ignore this topic?

For my part, I admit to a journey of discovery on the topic of spiritual gifts in the 21st century. My personal journey provides both a studies perspective and a great deal of grace for those who disagree with my position. When I first began reading passages relating to spiritual gifts I innocently assumed them to be teaching how God desires to work through His church. Things began muddled by two experiences. First, I saw a lack of real world examples. I read in the Bible about healing, words of wisdom, etc. However, in many Pentecostal/Charismatic churches what I experienced was much different. I received excellent teaching on the reality of spiritual gifts without anyone actually experiencing these gifts. It seemed to me that for many Pentecostals/Charismatics the real issue was being able to articulate a theological position rather than living out a biblical reality.

Second, I saw within some Pentecostal/Charismatic circles "spiritual exercises" which seemed at odds with the character of the Holy Spirit. Activities which caused division, and diverted people's attention from Jesus and placed it on themselves or upon the church leaders. While they claimed to be operating in the gifts of the Holy Spirit their focus was nowhere near anything I read in the Bible.

These two experiences took me for a place of believing in spiritual gifts for the modern church to a place of doubt. How could the Holy Spirit's gifts be for today when many of those claiming to believe in them are never seen operating in them? Worse yet, how could the Holy Spirit's gifts be for today when many of those claiming to believe in them appeared to be emotionally unstable or self-focused? I realize these are harsh statements. I don't mean to condemn anyone else. Rather, I am simply sharing my personal journey on the subject with you. For years I simply took the stance that the gifts of the Holy Spirit are available through churches today, yet, on an extremely limited or rare basis.

It wasn't until I began reexamining the topic several years ago that things came full circle for me. I had gone from believing the spiritual gifts were available to God's children to believing they were only available on rare occasion and back to believing they are available. There is a genuine need for the 21st century church to reexamine the validity, necessity, and operation of spiritual gifts within the church setting. Many have exchanged the genuine power of God for entertainment in an attempt to appear relevant. This change has filled many seats with bodies but left many souls hungry for the reality of God in their lives.

What follows is a simple examination of the text itself. I am not offering any denominational position or trying to push a personal agenda. This is simply a short look at what the Bible says on the topic. Whether or not you believe these are still in operation we can agree that the church saw them in operation in the first century. The book itself will be written in three sections:

- What the Bible teaches about the spiritual gifts coming to an end following first century (this will be the shortest section).

- What the Bible teaches about the operation of spiritual gifts within the church.

- The distinction between corporate spiritual gifts and personal baptism in the Holy Spirit.

Section One

What the Bible teaches about the spiritual gifts coming to an end following first century

Just a week before starting the manuscript for the book you're reading I was reminded, again, of its importance while attending a service. The speaker was passionate and committed to conveying our need for salvation. His style of preaching was the exact opposite of mine and yet he did a great job keeping our attention. Perhaps that says something about my style of preaching and its need for improvement but that's another issue entirely. During the sermons he randomly inserted a short segment against the Pentecostal/Charismatic movement. He said, "*All we need is the Bible*" (for the record I'm in total agreement with that statement). He then proceeded to say, "*We don't need speaking in tongues, we don't need miracles, we don't need healing! All we need is the Bible!*"

As I sat there listening to him resume his main point - that everyone needs salvation - I was struck by the irony of his statement. On the one hand he was totally correct in stating all we need is the Bible. However, I couldn't help but wonder what he meant by that statement. After all, the Bible we need contains many clear teachings on spiritual gifts. How can one need the Bible and yet deny the teachings contained within its pages?

Over the years I have attended many such seminars, heard sermons, read books, and talked with fellow ministers who've claimed that spiritual gifts no longer exist. To their credit each of these ministers value the operation of spiritual gifts during the first century as seen in the pages of the New Testament. However, they have a few different reasons why these spiritual gifts which they affirm as legitimate so long ago are no longer in operation today.

First, is the idea that the spiritual gifts only operated through the Apostles. Once the last Apostle, John, died at the end of the first century the Holy Spirit didn't continue these gifts. The issue I have with this includes passages like 1 Corinthians 12-14 (the focus of this book). As we will see in the second section of that book an Apostle (Paul) was writing to followers of Jesus and instructing them in how the Holy Spirit operates spiritual gifts through them (a bunch on non-apostles).

Second, is the concept that spiritual gifts were needed until the New Testament was written. Once it was completed in 95 or 96 AD there was no longer a need for spiritual gifts so they stopped. There are several issues with this idea but space only permits pointing out one contradiction with this view. It seems anti-productive to write so much about spiritual gifts in the New Testament only to suddenly and without warning remove them from operation.

Third, is the belief that all we need is the Bible. I actually heard this last week in a service I was attending. The minster said (like thousands of ministers before him) "We don't need speaking in tongues, we don't need miracles, we don't need spiritual gifts! All we need is the Bible!" On its surface nothing sounds more biblical than saying "All we need is the Bible." However, when we consider what the statement "all we need is the Bible" actually means, things change. The Bible, especially the New Testament, tells reading about spiritual gifts, miracles, and speaking in tongues. It also describes how these supernatural activities are to function within a healthy church. Therefore, when we

14

say "all we need is the Bible" aren't we stating that we need the teaching from its pages? Don't those pages teach about speaking in tongues, miracles, and spiritual gifts? I believe they do.

Rather than spending countless pages arguing with the reasons well intentioned people claim spiritual gifts no longer exist I thought I'd list all the scriptures which teach spiritual gifts are gone. The remainder of this section will be dedicated to a listing of all the passages showing spiritual gifts ceased at the end of the first century.

Here they are:

That's correct. The entire list of passages stating that spiritual gifts will cease at the close of the first century are zero. Nowhere in the New Testament are readers told the Holy Spirit will discontinue moving in His church through spiritual gifts at the close of the first century.

Section Two
What the Bible teaches about the operation of spiritual gifts within the church

Anyone who studies the topic of spiritual gifts understands the enormity of the subject. The New Testament is filled with teachings on spiritual gifts. For our purposes we will simply follow the single largest single section on the topic of spiritual gifts, 1 Corinthians chapters 12 through 14. This one section is not all the New Testament has to say on the topic. However, it will provide us with a clear foundational understanding for how the Holy Spirit works through spiritual gifts within His Church.

The longer I serve Jesus and work among other followers of Jesus the more valuable I find this extended teaching in 1 Corinthians 12-14. For those of us who call the Pentecostal/Charismatic movement our home we have seen the excesses and misapplications which prompted Paul to write these chapters centuries ago. Rather than give the numerous examples of the Holy Spirit providing spiritual gifts throughout the world today this book will simply focus on the 1 Corinthians' teaching about the subject laid out in chapters 12 through 14. This book will look at this extended discussion of spiritual gifts within the church by walking through each of the three chapters. Certainly much more can be said about each verse in these three chapters than will be stated here. The point of this book is simply to provide a working outline from scripture on the topic of spiritual gifts. For this reason much will be left unsaid in our attempt to provide a foundational teaching on spiritual gifts.

1 Corinthians 12

12:1-3 The Foundations For Effective Operation Is Spiritual Gifts

In the interest of full disclosure I must admit that one of my frustrations with spiritual gifts in the 21st century is that they can be so easily counterfeited. Dozens of examples can be provided of people "faking" spiritual gifts either for profit or to draw a following. The fact is that no one counterfeits something unless it has value. People counterfeit $100 bills because they have value. No one bothers to counterfeit a $3 bill because there is no value in it. The very fact that spiritual gifts are counterfeited by some adds to the proof of their genuine value. The other piece of good news is that counterfeiting spiritual gifts isn't a new phenomenon. In fact it traces its legacy back to the first century. Paul himself opens this extended section on legitimate spiritual gifts with a warning about counterfeit gifts.

Now concerning what comes from the Spirit: brothers, I do not want you to be unaware. You know that when you were pagans, you used to be led off to the idols that could not speak. Therefore I am informing you that no one speaking by the Spirit of God says, "Jesus is cursed," and no one can say, "Jesus is Lord," except by the Holy Spirit. - 1 Corinthians 12:1-3

Paul begins his discussion on the validity of spiritual gifts within the church by providing what should be obvious but, sadly, often is not. He provides us with this general principle: Spiritual gifts always promote Jesus. **Jesus is cursed** and **Jesus is Lord** aren't exact words someone operating in spiritual gifts necessarily uses. Rather, the entire message of one purporting to be led by the Holy Spirit must always promote Jesus. Those of us who've spent our adult lives within the Pentecostal/Charismatic community have seen examples of people promoting themselves, additional requirements, and even occult practices all in the name of God. I wish this were not true. The only good news here is that these diversions from promoting Jesus are nothing new. The first century church (which had the original Apostles as overseers) dealt with this issue.

One of the examples which always comes to my mind when I read these verses happened in the late 1980s. I was with friends at a special service taking place in a hotel ballroom. Things were moving along wonderfully until the main speaker (a famous minister whose name I will not include here) suddenly shifted from what he was teaching to provide a "prophetic word" just for us. Again, I do believe in the gift of prophecy within the church as did the Apostle Paul. What follows, however, is a prime example of "**Jesus be cursed**."

The exact words are now lost to time but I vividly recall the general sentiment. His basic prophetic word "just for us" was, "*God has a great spiritual promotion for you. It is His desire that your needs be more than met so you can live in financial abundance. Tonight the Holy Spirit wants you to step out in faith and provide the absolute best financial gift you can. He will use this gift as seed which will grow into your financial freedom.*" Sadly, many present that night followed his "prophetic word" and gave money needed for the necessities of life. Notice what happened in my example. He did not say "Jesus is cursed." He, however, did promote greed over obedience. He was telling us that God wanted us to be rich and that the way this provision would occur involved giving money that night specifically to him.

I use this example because in our culture it hardly seems "evil." At best it would be considered by many as misguided, opportunistic, or even sleazy perhaps but not evil. However, according to scripture (this passage and more like it) what was done was evil. This man, while purporting to speak on the Holy Spirit's behalf diverted people's focus from Jesus onto their own greed. Anything done in Jesus' name or by inspiration of the Holy Spirit that takes attention away from Jesus and puts it somewhere else is cursing Jesus. This is a foundational principle for the operation of any and all spiritual gifts.

A second example happened in the early 2000s. Honestly, I wouldn't believe it had I not been there to witness it myself. The minister was preaching and said the Holy Spirit had given him a word of knowledge concerning Jesus' words in John 10:34 ("You are gods"). He said the Holy Spirit showed him that all Christians are little gods and create reality, their own reality, just as God created the world in Genesis chapters 1 and 2. If we wanted a better personal world we just needed to command it into existence. Hopefully you see the obvious problems with such a statement. The key flaw (certainly not the only flaw) in this bad teaching is that our focus is pulled away from a humble reliance on Jesus and puts it firmly in our own abilities. Abilities, I might add, no human possesses.

Paul's point in these opening verses on spiritual gifts is simple. Anything that takes our attention away from Jesus is "cursing Jesus" and anything that puts our attention on Jesus is saying "Jesus is Lord." The purpose of spiritual gifts is ALWAYS to promote Jesus. Anything that promotes a particular person, ideology, or group rather than Jesus isn't a legitimate gift of the Holy Spirit.

12:4-11 Cooperation In Spiritual Gifts Within The Church
While most of us agree that the concept of 12:1-3 is still at work within the church today, some would argue (quite loudly at times) that verses 4-11 no longer have a place within God's church. Having already laid out my reasons why I believe they are still available to the church in the first section of this book let me show how you've been used to provide some of these gifts without even realizing it. I will not provide examples for each of the spiritual gifts listed here but the few examples should provide adequate evidence proving my point.

Now there are different gifts, but the same Spirit. There are different ministries, but the same Lord. And there are different activities, but the same God activates each gift in each person. A demonstration of the Spirit is given to each person to produce what is beneficial: to one is given a message of wisdom through the Spirit, to another, a message of knowledge by the same Spirit, to another, faith by the same Spirit, to another, gifts of healing by the one Spirit, to another, the performing of miracles, to another, prophecy, to another, distinguishing between spirits, to another, different kinds of languages, to another, interpretation of languages. But one and the same Spirit is active in all these,

distributing to each person as He wills. - 1 Corinthians 12:4-11

For the sake of space I will only mention a few of these spiritual gifts which you've likely experienced without realizing it. Before I do that, it's worth noting the phrase **message of** does mean a verbal message. These gifts within the church are designed to be spoken, either by one congregant to another or by a congregant to the group. It is also worth noting that they are individual gifts provided by the Holy Spirit for specific occasions. These are passing gifts rather than permanent gifts like evangelist, or pastor-teacher.

Now let's take a look at how God has provided you with these gifts.

Message of wisdom - Have you ever had one of those occasions when talking with someone and you knew the right path to take in a situation and it even surprised you? Often we will chalk it up to luck or intuition. However, you were most likely as a follower of Jesus being used in the gift of wisdom. Because this happens so "naturally" and so simply we often fail to see it as the spiritual gift God gives us. This personal experience of the gift of wisdom is often shared within the church setting for a larger good.

Message of knowledge - Have you ever offered advice to someone or "instinctively" knew why a person was in their situation without them giving clues? I mean the type of advice that even amazes you when it comes out of your mouth. The type of advice that makes you pause because it was so perfect for the circumstance and you had no idea where it came from. On those occasions you are being used in the gift of knowledge. Again, it flows so "naturally" that we often mistakenly give credit to everything but a gift of the Holy Spirit. This personal experience of the gift of knowledge is often shared within the church setting for the greater good.

Faith - This is not faith to believe the gospel message. This is a unique gift provided by the Holy Spirit to believe God for things others have given up believing to happen. A great example of this is a friend of mine who believed God for a certain circumstance to change. Someone asked my friend how they could believe God for this when "obviously" He wasn't going to change the circumstance. My friend responded simply "*I just know as certainly as I'm standing here that God will do this.*" A few years later God did just that. The gift of believing in the face of such obvious reasons to doubt is the spiritual gift of faith. It provided my friend with the strength to trust God when no one else could.

Distinguishing between spirits - Have you ever met someone (especially in a church setting) and instantly knew they were trouble and to be avoided? I don't mean after you've loaned them $1,000.00 and they moved away and changed their phone number. This is the gift of distinguishing between spirits and the Holy Spirit provides it to protect us from those we would otherwise fall prey to later. This personal experience of distinguishing of spirits is often shared within a church setting. However, nearly 30 years of ministry experience has shown me a person is safest exercising this gift within a church setting by going to the leadership with this insight rather than posting warnings on a bulletin board.

Here's a quick definition of the remaining gifts Paul mentions to the church in this passage:

Gifts of healing - The Holy Spirit healing people because we prayed for them.

Performing of miracles - A quick read through the book of Acts provides a glimpse of how this gift operates. Things which are contrary to the natural order occur for the benefit of people.

Prophecy - A word of edification, encouragement, or consolation (1 Corinthians 14:3) spoken to a person or a congregation in their known language. It will never contradict the Bible.

Different kinds of languages - A message spoken to a congregation in a language the speaker didn't learn. 1 Corinthians 14 gives great instruction on the use of this gift.

Interpreting of languages - An interpretation of the message spoken in a different language within the congregation. Because different languages and interpretation of those languages work together 1 Corinthians 14 gives a great deal of instruction on the process and purpose of interpretation.

These nine items are spiritual gifts provided by the Holy Spirit for the benefit of Jesus' church. They are designed to assist the church, keep it healthy, remind it of Jesus' concern, and to protect it from people with deceptive motives. At the top of the list of gifts getting all the attention by people in the 21st century are tongues/interpretation and prophecy. Those against spiritual gifts today say tongues and interpretation no longer exist and that prophecy here means preaching.

The great difficulty with prophecy meaning preaching is that one must do several twists of scripture to make that opinion viable. It is one thing to say all the gifts are extinct (a wrong thing of course but at least it's an honest approach). It is another thing entirely to transform Paul's use of prophecy here to mean preaching. I will focus only on one key problem here. The main problem with this approach is that one must then retranslate the term prophecy everywhere else in the New Testament to mean preaching. A quick trace through the Gospels and book of Acts will show how messy such an approach becomes.

Prophecy within this context, as in the Gospels and Acts, is the shortened version of tongues and interpretation. Think of it like driving. Recently I went with a group of friends from St. Louis to Greenville, KY to work at Set Free Mission Bible Training Center for the week. On the way down we took mainly back roads. It took longer but we got there. On the way home we took mainly the highway. The highway was about two hours faster than the back roads but both routes took us to our destination. Prophecy is like taking a highway in that it gets you to your destination quickly. It is a person speaking a message of edification, encouragement, or consolation to another in the congregation or to the entire congregation (1 Corinthians 14:3).

Tongues and interpretation is similar to taking the back roads. It gets to the same destination but takes longer. One person will speak in a language unknown to the majority of listeners then someone else will provide its meaning in their language. On occasions the same person will provide both the tongues and the interpretation. You can see how this is a slower means to the same end as prophecy.

Be it prophecy (the highway) or tongues and interpretation (the longer route to the same destination) the principle of 1 Corinthians 14:3 applies equally. These are gifts given to benefit God's people rather than to belittle them. I've heard the type of messages which promoted a speaker more than they did Jesus. I've heard the type of messages used as a godly disguise for pent up anger and resentment against others. These false messages fall squarely under Paul's warning about Jesus being cursed. They do not, however, mean the real doesn't exist.

Saying you don't want God to use these gifts in your life or church because of the counterfeit that exist is like saying you don't want to be given money because there is counterfeit money out there. We all know counterfeit money exists but I doubt seriously that any of us have burned our cash simply because fake money may be out there. Paul's teaching in 1 Corinthians 12:1-3 gives us the means by which we can judge the real from the counterfeit. This standard is given because God wants us to use the real and reject the fake.

1 Corinthians 12:12-27 Humility In Spiritual Gifts Within The Church

A 100 years ago while attending college I got a campus job working construction. It didn't pay well but the job was on campus and worked with my class schedule. Most of us had very little idea what we were doing and learned on the job. If time allowed I could give dozens of hilarious examples of why most of us who made so little were probably still overpaid.

Some of the student/workers had construction skills and others of us (myself included) had no applicable skills. However, we were all paid equally and learned to work together for the common goal. One reason for throwing us all together on a construction project so we could learn from each other. It did mean the project took longer because skilled workers had to slowly train us unskilled workers. However, great friendships were developed and those of us unfamiliar with construction learned from those who came to the project with skills. Those college days remind me of the humility Paul states we need in this section regarding the gifts of the Holy Spirit.

For as the body is one and has many parts, and all the parts of that body, though many, are one body— so also is Christ. For we were all baptized by one Spirit into one body—whether Jews or Greeks, whether slaves or free—and we were all made to drink of one Spirit. So the body is not one part but many. If the foot should say, "Because I'm not a hand, I don't belong to the body," in spite of this it still belongs to the body. And if the ear should say, "Because I'm not an eye, I don't belong to the

body," in spite of this it still belongs to the body. If the whole body were an eye, where would the hearing be? If the whole body were an ear, where would the sense of smell be? But now God has placed each one of the parts in one body just as He wanted. And if they were all the same part, where would the body be? Now there are many parts, yet one body. So the eye cannot say to the hand, "I don't need you!" Or again, the head can't say to the feet, "I don't need you!" But even more, those parts of the body that seem to be weaker are necessary. And those parts of the body that we think to be less honorable, we clothe these with greater honor, and our unpresentable parts have a better presentation. But our presentable parts have no need of clothing. Instead, God has put the body together, giving greater honor to the less honorable, so that there would be no division in the body, but that the members would have the same concern for each other. So if one member suffers, all the members suffer with it; if one member is honored, all the members rejoice with it. Now you are the body of Christ, and individual members of it. - 1 Corinthians 12:12-27

Paul deals with two responses to spiritual gifts which are just as present in the 21st century as they were in the 1st century. They are jealousy and pride. Using the body as a metaphor Paul states the purpose for Jesus' church. The purpose of the church is to bring people who normally would have nothing in common into a place where they learn to live in unity and mutual respect. When a church of dissimilar people can live in unity because of Jesus it becomes a testimony to the reality of Jesus Himself. Unity in the church is a witness to the world. In Paul's day the big issue was Jews and Gentile's living in unity within the church. This church was filled with people of different backgrounds, different values, different forms of entertainment, etc. However, because of their common faith in Jesus these things were set aside for the sake of unity. This was a powerful witness to the unsaved world to the reality of Jesus. Yet, jealousy and pride threatened to destroy this unity at every turn. In our passage the threat grew out of the operation of the gifts of the Holy Spirit.

The first half of this section shows the jealousy which can occur because of the gifts of the Holy Spirit. Because it is God's choice how, when, where, and why the gifts of the Holy Spirit are distributed, jealousy was always a temptation. You can easily imagine someone thinking "*Why that Jew instead of me as a Gentile?*" or "*Why did God use that Gentile instead of me as a Jew?*" When God chose to use someone another didn't think worthy of such a gift, jealousy was at work. Paul goes on to note that this jealousy is manifested in one's belief that they weren't as important to God as the ones being used in the gifts of the Holy Spirit. In this case, what is provided as a means to bring greater unity and blessing to the church was corrupted to bring disunity through jealousy.

The cure for this jealousy is not to abandon the gifts of the Holy Spirit. Rather the cure is to grow in our relationship with Jesus and develop a greater sense of humility. After all there is a God and we are not Him. We are part of the church but only Jesus is the star of the church. Some congregations have banned expressions of the gifts so no one feels out of place or that someone else in the church is being used more than everyone else. This is akin to banning corporate worship because someone sings better than someone else and there may be hurt feelings over song selection. The issue is never who is or isn't being used at a particular moment to glorify Jesus. The issue is each of us needing to grow in humility.

The last half of this section deals with the opposite reaction to a manifestation of spiritual gifts. It is the issue of pride. Going back to my college construction job on campus I can provide great examples of pride causing problems. There were those skilled guys who took great pains to regularly remind the rest of us that they were more skilled than us. Their attitude brought division and a general sense of discomfort for those who had to work alongside them. One funny example of pride I like to use involved an air gun. This air gun drove long nails through thick boards with the simple pull of the trigger. It had a safety feature that wouldn't allow the gun to fire this long nail unless the barrel was pressed against the wood. Like most safety features there is a way to bypass it if someone looked hard enough. I was working with a skilled guy who loved reminding the rest of us how lucky we were to have him there. He made it known that we needed him but he did not need us. Showing off one day he put his finger over the safety feature to show us how to shoot the nail gun at a coffee cup across the room. In the process of showing off his superior knowledge he shot the tip of his pointer finger off.

This is exactly the attitude Paul is describing in the second half of our passage. Pride not only causes others to feel less important to the overall task of God's mission in the world. It also is dangerous to those who believe they are special to God. In my 30 years of ministry I have lost count of the number of people whom God used but ended up doing great damage to themselves, their families, their congregations because of their pride. They came to believe that God was using them in the spiritual gifts because there was something intrinsically special about them. The result of their pride caused them to make foolish decisions which impacted their lives in horrible ways.

The spiritual gifts are given to promote Jesus. In a congregation filled with different people learning to live in unity and humility they also function as an opportunity for us to grow in that humility. Spiritual gifts give us occasions to thank God for using those we may not have chosen. Spiritual gifts not only help the church directly (healing, prophecy, etc.) they help the church indirectly by giving each of us opportunity to deal with jealousy and pride.

1 Corinthians 12:28-31 Purpose Of Spiritual Gifts In The Church

Occasionally over the years I have come across well meaning but misguided followers of Jesus who are overly focused on the spiritual gifts. They run from conference to conference, church to church, event to event hoping to experience the next great spiritual event. Their focus is not on Jesus, it is not on living out their faith in a community of believers. Their focus is not even on sharing the good news with the unsaved. Their focus is built squarely upon seeing spiritual gifts in action. Paul is clear all the way through this extended teaching of 1 Corinthians 12 through 14 that such an attitude is wrong. It diminishes the true value of spiritual gifts and turns them into something akin to entertainment.

And God has placed these in the church: first apostles, second prophets, third teachers, next miracles, then gifts of healing, helping, managing, various kinds of languages. Are all apostles? Are all prophets? Are all teachers? Do all do miracles? Do all have gifts of healing? Do all speak in other languages? Do all interpret? But desire the greater gifts. And I will show you an even better way. - 1 Corinthians 12:28-31

It is worth noting that some see this section as proof Paul was preparing the church for an end to spiritual gifts. They propose that Paul is reminding them that God started with apostles, prophets and, teachers. This view falsely teaches that to show the validity of their message God added spiritual gifts. However, now Paul was preparing them for the day when God no longer needed spiritual gifts because they would trust the apostles, prophets, and teachers at their word. To be clear one cannot legitimately get such a view from this text. It simply is impossible for a number of reasons. Let me quickly give only three.

First, one must twist these verses into unrecognizable shapes to force such an interpretation. This section says exactly what it says. Forcing it to say God will soon stop providing spiritual gifts takes a great deal of effort. In fact, it takes more faith to believe this misunderstanding of the text than it does to simply believe the text itself.

Second, it makes no sense at all for Paul to spend three chapters discussing how the church should use spiritual gifts and here say *"Don't worry about it because soon you won't have them."* That would mean most of these three chapters would be a waste of time for everyone - for him to write and for them to read. It is like spending hours telling your child they need to study for a math test but then throw in a random statement like *"Don't worry about it because that test may not happen."* These mixed messages make no sense.

Third, such a belief - that the gifts were designed to prop up individuals - is an incorrect focus on both the spiritual gifts and on ministers. It says in essence that the power of the gospel wasn't strong enough to transform lives back then. If the gospel is powerful enough now, 20 centuries after Jesus walked the earth, without spiritual gifts accompanying it (and to be clear IT IS) then it certainly would have been equally as powerful in the first century. Nowhere in the New Testament does one read the power of the gospel isn't enough. In fact, the exact opposite is stated in places like Romans 1:16.

This short section provides again Paul's teaching on the purpose of spiritual gifts. They do not exist for entertainment and they are not given outside of people. Paul provides in this list an understanding that the spiritual gifts do not supersede the human connection. Apostles, prophets, and teachers (regardless of whatever else those offices do) focus the congregation's attention on the word of God. Paul is giving a reminder that spiritual gifts are NOT the focus of a congregation. Rather, the word of God is the central focus of a healthy congregation.

With this noted by Paul he also makes it clear that spiritual gifts are not to be ignored within the congregation. Spiritual gifts have a place within the life of a congregation and they are to be grounded in and work in partnership with the proclamation of scripture. My father puts it this way:

> A church built only on the Word dries up.
> A church built only on gifts blows up.
> A church built on the Word and the gifts grows up.

What follows is a generalization. There are wonderful examples of churches which defy this generalization. However, generalizations work because they are generally true. There are churches that focus on teaching the Bible while ignoring spiritual gifts. Often they are rigid and focused on proving their points more than they are focused on the joy Jesus provides. There are also churches which focus on experiencing spiritual gifts while ignoring the clear teaching of scripture regarding order. They can be exciting places but their level of spiritual maturity is almost nonexistent. Thankfully, there are an increasing number of congregations that their focus on teaching the scripture includes openness to the spiritual gifts. This combination of honoring Jesus by learning the Bible and being open to the Holy Spirit's gifts produces a wonderful environment for growth. There are exceptions to this generalization to be sure. However, I believe them to be the exception rather than the rule.

Here in chapter 12 Paul laid out the foundation for effectively using spiritual gifts, cooperation in spiritual gifts within the church, humility in spiritual gifts within the church, and the purpose of spiritual gifts within the church. In this last line of chapter 12 Paul prepares us for more teaching on spiritual gifts by stating "**And I will show you an even better way.**"

1 Corinthians 13

I've often wondered how many followers of Jesus would even know this chapter existed if it weren't for weddings and ecumenical services. This "love chapter" is incorporated into those moments of uniting people in marriage and congregations in special services. There is a place for this chapter to be used at such moments to be certain. However, if we view chapter 13 as a break in the action between chapters 12 and 14 we miss the power of this chapter all together. This isn't a break in the action where Paul is somehow saying "*Hey guys. You may not like this but remember we all have to love each other so be nice to me when I next see you.*" Paul, under the inspiration of the Holy Spirit, is strategically placing this section here. This chapter - chapter 13 - is part of Paul's teaching on spiritual gifts within the congregation.

1 Corinthians 13:1-8 Motivation For Proper Operations In Spiritual Gifts

Love is a word which is widely misunderstood in the modern church. It is preached about, written about, but not fully grasped because we often use the wrong definition. Many view love from the street perspective rather than the biblical one. The street form of love, in its base form, is defined as "*I'll like you if you're nice to me.*" Biblical love - the love defined in 1 Corinthians 13 - is "choosing to do what is in another's best interest." Street love is performance based and biblical love is choice based. Biblical love says "*I'll do what is best for you regardless of how you make me feel.*" It is this biblical love that Paul says should be the motivation for the use of spiritual gifts.

If I speak human or angelic languages but do not have love, I am a sounding gong or a clanging cymbal. If I have the gift of prophecy and understand all mysteries and all knowledge, and if I have all faith so that I can move mountains but do not have love, I am nothing. And if I donate all my goods to feed the poor, and if I give my body in order to boast but do not have love, I gain nothing. Love is patient, love is kind. Love does not envy, is not boastful, is not conceited, does not act improperly, is not selfish, is not provoked, and does not keep a record of wrongs. Love finds no joy in unrighteousness but rejoices in the truth. It bears all things, believes all things, hopes all things, endures all things. Love never ends. But as for prophecies, they will come to an end; as for languages, they will cease; as for knowledge, it will come to an end. - 1 Corinthians 13:-8

We should never divorce chapter 13 from chapters 12 and 14. When we do this the power of chapter 13 is lost all together. He begins this section with an honest appraisal of spiritual gifts without genuine love for others. Starting with the phrase **If I speak human or angelic languages.** This phrase can only mean one thing within the context of chapters 12 and 14 - tongues and interpretation. Don't misunderstand me here. Many have tried with great diligence to make it mean something else. However, trying to redefine its meaning doesn't actually change Paul's original meaning. Because this chapter is set in the middle of the listing of tongues and interpretation (chapter 12) and an extended teaching on tongues and interpretation (chapter14) these chapters must become our guides for their interpretation.

Some have defined human or angelic languages to mean poor articulation (human) and excellent articulation (angelic) when preaching. An even smaller group has even used it to separate women's speech from men's speech in church. They say human language refers to a woman speaking to a church and angelic language refers to when men, anointed as preachers, speak to a church. Even if you choose to agree with the first false interpretation of the passage I hope you choose to reject the second outright.

Paul moves into an extensive teaching on tongues and interpretation in the next chapter. Here he is setting the foundation or the motivation from which a person should operate in these gifts. With that noted I believe the most natural way to interpret this phrase - **If I speak human or angelic languages** - is to take it at face value. In other words, the Holy Spirit will provide a person a message for the church in either an unknown human language or in an unknown language of angels. Because the speaker doesn't know the language he/she has no idea which it is they are speaking.

In the middle of this section Paul gives us the basic character traits of biblical love. They are vastly different from street level love. It is motivated to better the recipient of that love. It is a matter of choice born out of humility. It is utterly contrary to what the unsaved can offer. Years back I was on an outreach trip with friends. We met, and watched God use, a man in the gift of prophecy. God was genuinely using him to minister to the needs of those present. However, behind the scenes he was quite arrogant. He viewed himself as too important to help with the work projects and voiced his opinion that he should be first in line at meals. His obvious lack of biblical love did a lot to undermine the good brought through him by the Holy Spirit during the services. Biblical love as the motivation for our lives enhances the validity of spiritual gifts. It is a lifestyle we should all strive to convey.

A more natural way to read the text is in the context of eternity. Here on earth the Holy Spirit has provided us with the spiritual gifts to benefit us. However, in heaven we will no longer need these spiritual gifts. When we move from this life to the next these gifts, so needed now, will no longer be necessary. Love however, is needed on this side of eternity and the other side. The final statement in this section of Paul's reminds us of our need to be humble (**Love never ends. But as for prophecies, they will come to an end; as for**

languages, they will cease; as for knowledge, it will come to an end). Our opinions on scripture are not the final statement on them. Only the scriptures are complete in their message. When the Holy Spirit uses us in the spiritual gifts they are not complete. Only the written text of scripture promises to be a complete word on any subject.

1 Corinthians 13:9-12 Humility In The Operation Of Spiritual Gifts

The importance of love as the base of operating in the spiritual gifts simply cannot be overstated. One of the purposes of the spiritual gifts is to promote Jesus' right to use whomever He wants. The one being used on that occasion isn't the star. Rather, it is the Jesus who should take center stage. Remember, that God can use anyone or anything he wishes. A quick reading of Numbers 22:21-39 should make this evident.

For we know in part, and we prophesy in part. But when the perfect comes, the partial will come to an end. When I was a child, I spoke like a child, I thought like a child, I reasoned like a child. When I became a man, I put aside childish things. For now we see indistinctly, as in a mirror, but then face to face. Now I know in part, but then I will know fully, as I am fully known. - 1 Corinthians 13:9-12

Paul ends this section with the opening sentence: "**But as for prophecies, they will come to an end; as for languages, they will cease; as for knowledge, it will come to an end.**" Some have tried to use these two sentences to incorrectly teach that tongues, interpretation, and prophecy have ceased. However, if we allow the Bible to speak for itself we cannot accept such an interpretation as valid. If this means tongues, interpretations, and prophecy have ceased then so must, by default, has knowledge. How can it be that knowledge is promised to cease along with the others yet it somehow remains alone? It simply doesn't make sense to view it this way. According to Paul's writing here tongues, interpretation, and prophecy will remain until knowledge also ceases.

True spiritual maturity isn't seen in the operation of spiritual gifts but in the attitude of biblical love. Children are characterized by being self-centered. They want their toys, their snacks, and their way regardless of any inconvenience it causes others around them. A child's world revolves around the child's desires. As a child grows into an adult they should learn to consider the needs of others. As an aside, we've all met adults who failed to learn this important lesson. This biblical type of love marks the difference between a child and an adult. Paul says that a spiritual adult **puts aside childish things**. He/She no longer lives for their ego, desire for acknowledgment, or feelings of self-importance as the driving force of their life. Rather, he/she focuses on being a benefit to others.

This section ends with the clear recognition that we don't fully understand God's plan, especially when it comes to who He chooses to use in the distribution of spiritual gifts. He states, **For now we see indistinctly, as in a mirror, but then face to face. Now I know in part, but then I will know fully, as I am fully known**. When we ask ourselves, or God, why someone "like them" would be used in a particular spiritual gift it is a sign that we don't fully know God's plan. One of the reasons God uses those we wouldn't have chosen on particular occasions is precisely, in part, to remind us that God's plan is bigger than we are able to comprehend. When we stand before God we will fully know His plan as plainly as He now fully knows us. Until that moment we demonstrate spiritual maturity by rejoicing with those God uses and thanking Him for ministering spiritual gifts to the church.

1 Corinthians 13:13. Foundation For Effective Operation In Spiritual Gifts

One of the oddest places I remember this last verse of 1 Corinthians 13 being quoted was at a funeral. I've become so used to hearing it at weddings that it took me by surprise when the minister chose it for the main text of the funeral sermon. I will say that he did a brilliant job using it to show the value of how we are remembered in the thought of those we leave behind. However, Paul's main purpose for including it was in relation to spiritual gifts.

Now these three remain: faith, hope, and love. But the greatest of these is love. - 1 Corinthians 13:13

It is highly doubtful that Paul had weddings or funerals in mind when he penned this last line. Rather, Paul's focus was on spiritual gifts. **Faith** and **hope** sustain us through difficult times. They allow us to trust God even when we don't understand what He is doing at the time. However, there is a time coming when these two great sustaining virtues will no longer be needed. When we stand before Jesus in the next life we will fully understand each of the events of our lives we experience here and now. We will simply no longer need faith or hope in the next life. Who needs faith or hope for what they already have?

However, **love** transcends this life and the next. Love, biblical love, is so foundational to every aspect of our lives that it will continue to exist in the next life. Precisely because of the transcendent nature of love's quality Paul wants us to focus on it in this life. When followers of Jesus live out biblical love the spiritual gifts cannot become a source of contention or difficulty. Biblical love is the foundation which allows the spiritual gifts to have their greatest impact on our lives. It is the foundation of biblical love which makes the church's testimony to the reality of Jesus valid in an unsaved world operating in street level love.

In this great passage about love Paul tells us the motivation for proper operations in spiritual gifts, the need for humility in the operations of spiritual gifts, and the foundation of biblical love when operating in spiritual gifts. Chapter 13 is the linchpin to insure that spiritual gifts remain in their proper place. They are not to become the focal point of church life. Nor are they to be dismissed out of hand.

1 Corinthians 14

1 Corinthians 14:1-5 Prophesy And Tongues In Church Services
Something the 21st century church has in common with the 1st century church is it's fascination with tongues/interpretation and prophecy. Anyone who has

spent much time in the Pentecostal/Charismatic movement has experienced genuine messages from the Holy Spirit through these means. Having laid out for us the basic truth about spiritual gifts in chapter 12 and the underling character trait needed for spiritual gifts to function meaningfully in chapter 13 Paul now turns to concerns over the verbal gifts of tongues/interpretation and prophecy within a church setting.

Pursue love and desire spiritual gifts, and above all that you may prophesy. For the person who speaks in another language is not speaking to men but to God, since no one understands him; however, he speaks mysteries in the Spirit. But the person who prophesies speaks to people for edification, encouragement, and consolation. The person who speaks in another language builds himself up, but he who prophesies builds up the church. I wish all of you spoke in other languages, but even more that you prophesied. The person who prophesies is greater than the person who speaks in languages, unless he interprets so that the church may be built up. - 1 Corinthians 14:1-5

For Paul chapter 14 isn't a new line of thought separate from chapter 13. Rather, it is a continuation of the topic. This is clear in the first line - **Pursue love and desire spiritual gifts**. One is active (pursue) and the other passive (desire). Great difficulties arise when followers of Jesus switch these two and begin pursuing (active) spiritual gifts and desiring (passive) love. Our focus is always to actively pursue love. We are to seek out ways we can grow in and more adequately express biblical love to others. Spiritual gifts are passive in that we can do nothing to make them happen. There is no "priming the pump" to make spiritual gifts flow. They are always and in every instance gifts from the Holy Spirit.

Paul begins with a statement that we should desire to prophecy above speaking in a language we haven't learned. While there are those who teach Paul doesn't want us to speak in languages we've never learned such a thing from Paul himself. In this chapter Paul has much to say about the validity of speaking in languages he/she has not learned. His opening statements on the topic reveal the love factor which was the focus of chapter 13. These verbal spiritual gifts within the church setting are for the greater good. It is obvious (or at least it should be obvious) that hearing a message in one's own language has greater impact than hearing a language one doesn't understand.

Notice though that Paul does not say unknown languages are without value. Paul says that a person who speaks in a language he/she hasn't learned engages in two very important activities:

Speaking to God.
Building himself/herself up.

Where in the Bible does it state speaking to God or building up oneself is ever incorrect or selfish? These are two wonderful gifts which God provides to His children. They are only wrong when used at an inappropriate time. It is inappropriate, according to Paul, to speak in tongues in a church setting unless **he interprets so that the church may be built up**. Evidently some in the 1st century church were using their private prayer/worship language in the public setting of church. This was an appropriate personal worship shared in an inappropriate way and causing confusion.

As an aside, the last section of this book will focus on the personal gift of praying and worshiping in a language the Holy Spirit provides. For now we will stay focused on the gifts of prophecy and tongues within the church setting.

Unless one also interprets in a known language what is spoken in an unknown language it is not appropriate. Notice that Paul gives us guidelines for understanding which prophetic words and which tongues/interpretations are valid. He states that God will speak to **people for edification, encouragement, and consolation**. According to Paul harsh words do not come from the Holy Spirit in prophecy or tongues/interpretations. Any time someone claims to be speaking on the Holy Spirit's behalf and the message doesn't follow this guideline he/she is operating in the counterfeit. The purpose of these verbal gifts is always, always, always, always, always to build up the congregation. They are never to tear down the congregation.

1 Corinthians 14:6-19 Tongues Used Properly In Church Services
Because of the possibility of causing confusion within a church setting many in Pentecostal/Charismatic church leadership have set policies that no verbal spiritual gifts (tongues/interpretations or prophecy) should take place

in the main service. They promote other gifts, namely gifts of healing, while discouraging verbal gifts. While discussing the issue with one such group of leaders this is the passage used to defend their position. I found it odd, as I do today, that a passage used to promote the verbal gifts would be used to silence them. Though I have not statistics as proof I privately wonder if the real issue for such leaders isn't an unspoken need to control everything that happens within the church setting.

But now, brothers, if I come to you speaking in other languages, how will I benefit you unless I speak to you with a revelation or knowledge or prophecy or teaching? Even inanimate things that produce sounds—whether flute or harp—if they don't make a distinction in the notes, how will what is played on the flute or harp be recognized? In fact, if the trumpet makes an unclear sound, who will prepare for battle? In the same way, unless you use your tongue for intelligible speech, how will what is spoken be known? For you will be speaking into the air. There are doubtless many different kinds of languages in the world, and all have meaning. Therefore, if I do not know the meaning of the language, I will be a foreigner to the speaker, and the speaker will be a foreigner to me. So also you— since you are zealous for spiritual gifts, seek to excel in building up the church. Therefore the person who speaks in another language should pray that he can interpret. For if I pray in another language, my spirit prays, but my understanding is unfruitful. What then? I will pray with the spirit, and I will also pray with my understanding. I will sing with the spirit, and I will also sing with my

understanding. Otherwise, if you praise with the spirit, how will the uninformed person say "Amen" at your giving of thanks, since he does not know what you are saying? For you may very well be giving thanks, but the other person is not being built up. I thank God that I speak in other languages more than all of you; yet in the church I would rather speak five words with my understanding, in order to teach others also, than 10,000 words in another language. - 1 Corinthians 14:6-19

Paul's emphasis here is rooted in 1 Corinthians 12 and 13. Spiritual gifts are given by God to benefit the group as a whole. The goal is never the expression of a spiritual gift itself. Rather, the goal is to benefit people through the proper use of these gifts at the proper time and in the proper way. Paul begins by noting the goal is to benefit people with a revelation, knowledge, prophetic word, or teaching. These are great goals. He goes on to say that these only benefit people if those present understand what is said. In other words, when (and it does happen occasionally today as it did in the 1st century) someone speaks in a language they haven't learned without an interpretation it is actually anti productive. Contrary to what some teach, Paul is not saying tongues/interpretation have no place in the church. Rather, Paul is saying they are not an end unto themselves.

Unlike many in the 21st century church Paul was not anti spiritual gifts. He states clearly here "**since you are zealous for spiritual gifts, seek to excel in building up the church**." Paul does not chastise people for spiritual gifts. Nor does he state they will cease soon.

Paul says use spiritual gifts properly for the benefit of the church. When, in a church setting, a message is given in an unlearned language the speaker of that message should pray that God will also give him/her the interpretation of that message. Both must be shared or else what would have been a blessing becomes a spectacle.

Paul adds this amazing truth on tongues when he says, **"I will pray with the spirit, and I will also pray with my understanding. I will sing with the spirit, and I will also sing with my understanding. Otherwise, if you praise with the spirit, how will the uninformed person say "Amen" at your giving of thanks, since he does not know what you are saying? For you may very well be giving thanks, but the other person is not being built up."** Within a church setting a message in tongues has legitimate benefit for the congregation when followed by an interpretation in a known language. Often, according to 1 Corinthians chapter 12 one person gives the unknown message and another provides the interpretation of that message. However, the responsibility for interpreting falls upon the speaker of that unlearned language. Again, Paul isn't saying "*Silly people. Stop this public tongues stuff. It's no longer part of what God is doing in the church.*" Rather, Paul is saying messages in tongues should be followed by interpretation. These should be done at the proper time in a service to be valid. Both must take place for the church to be edified.

This section to the 1st century church, and by default to the 21st century church, shows a distinction between private worship and public worship. Paul is clear when he says he regularly prays privately in a language he didn't learn. However, in a church setting this gift is used far less than a known language. Paul is not saying unknown languages have no value. In fact, he indicates they have great value in private prayer and worship. All Paul is saying here is that within the context of public worship tongues are not the focal point. Edifying God's children is the focal point and the primary way this occurs is through a language everyone understands.

1 Corinthians 14:20-25 The Place Of Tongues And Prophecy In Church Services
One of the church's great concerns is the introduction of Jesus to unbelievers. Any congregation which neglects this vital portion of its mission is showing signs of spiritual neglect. The spiritual gifts, when used properly, are one avenue of evangelism for the church to reach unbelievers.

Brothers, don't be childish in your thinking, but be infants in regard to evil and adult in your thinking. It is written in the law: I will speak to these people by people of other languages and by the lips of foreigners, and even then, they will not listen to Me, says the Lord. It follows that speaking in other languages is intended as a sign, not for believers but for unbelievers. But prophecy is not for unbelievers but for believers. Therefore, if the whole church assembles together and all are speaking in other languages and people who are uninformed or unbelievers come in, will they not say that you are out of your minds? But if all are

prophesying and some unbeliever or uninformed person comes in, he is convicted by all and is judged by all. The secrets of his heart will be revealed, and as a result he will fall facedown and worship God, proclaiming, "God is really among you." - 1 Corinthians 14:20-25

Paul quotes Isaiah 28:11, 12 in making the connection between tongues and the unbeliever. There are some well meaning followers of Jesus who believe (as some seemed to believe in the 1st century church) that speaking in tongues alone is an adequate witness to the reality of Jesus. I once spoke with a gentleman who couldn't understand why his unsaved family members thought his church was insane. As we talked I discovered that his church regularly had extended times (up to 30 minutes) when people would take turns just speaking or singing in a language they never learned. Rarely was there an interpretation of the messages. As politely as possible I walked him through this section of scripture. While the congregation he attended still participates in that odd activity he has moved to a more biblically based church. A Pentecostal/Charismatic congregation which properly operates in the spiritual gifts becomes a door through which the unsaved can meet Jesus for themselves.

The focus of this Isaiah passage quoted by Paul as that part of the proof Israel wasn't in proper relationship with Him would be that they couldn't understand those around them. It has marks of the results God brought from the building of the tower in Genesis 11. Paul's point is that the Holy Spirit's ability to speak through people in an unknown language is a sign they are not in a proper relationship with Him. Within the church setting, messages in an unknown language are a sign they don't understand God. It is the message in the known language - either an interpretation or prophecy - that confirms the reality of God to the unsaved.

I find it odd that a church, whose mission includes evangelism to the unsaved - would fail to use all the tools available. Messages in unknown languages alone are not evangelism. However, messages in unknown languages accompanied by an interpretation in a known language or prophecy can be a powerful evangelism tool.

Paul is clear about the evangelistic power of the verbal spiritual gifts when used properly. He states here, "**But if all are prophesying and some unbeliever or uninformed person comes in, he is convicted by all and is judged by all. The secrets of his heart will be revealed, and as a result he will fall facedown and worship God, proclaiming, "God is really among you**." The Holy Spirit will often use verbal spiritual gifts to convict an unbeliever of sin and draw them to Jesus. When dealing with Paul's teaching on spiritual gifts (as with any biblical teaching) it is important to remember the entire text and not focus solely on one or two verses. That is the case here. Paul isn't saying the Holy Spirit will speak and say "*Bob on the fifth row is an unbeliever and has been cheating on his taxes.*" Paul stated earlier that legitimate prophecy and tongues/interpretation is marked by edification, encouragement, and consolation. It is through these messages of God's goodness that the unsaved are drawn by the Holy Spirit to Jesus.

1 Corinthians 14:26-40 Spiritual Gifts Exist For A Purpose Beyond Themselves

The first two verses of this extended teaching (1 Corinthians 12:1, 2) began with the purpose of spiritual gifts within the church. Paul ends this discussion with an extended form of the same thought. Spiritual gifts have a place within the church and their proper use is found in a purpose beyond the gifts themselves.

What then is the conclusion, brothers? Whenever you come together, each one has a psalm, a teaching, a revelation, another language, or an interpretation. All things must be done for edification. If any person speaks in another language, there should be only two, or at the most three, each in turn, and someone must interpret. But if there is no interpreter, that person should keep silent in the church and speak to himself and to God. Two or three prophets should speak, and the others should evaluate. But if something has been revealed to another person sitting there, the first prophet should be silent. For you can all prophesy one by one, so that everyone may learn and everyone may be encouraged. And the prophets' spirits are under the control of the prophets, since God is not a God of disorder but of peace. As in all the churches of the saints, the women should be silent in the churches, for they are not permitted to speak, but should be submissive, as the law also says. And if they want to learn something, they should ask their own husbands at home, for it is disgraceful for a woman to speak in the church meeting. Did the word of God originate

from you, or did it come to you only? If anyone thinks he is a prophet or spiritual, he should recognize that what I write to you is the Lord's command. But if anyone ignores this, he will be ignored. Therefore, my brothers, be eager to prophesy, and do not forbid speaking in other languages. But everything must be done decently and in order. - 1 Corinthians 14:26-40

Here we have some practical instructions on proper use and motivations regarding spiritual gifts. He begins this closing section with an outstanding statement: "**What then is the conclusion, brothers? Whenever you come together, each one has a psalm, a teaching, a revelation, another language, or an interpretation. All things must be done for edification.**" So excited about Jesus was the 1st century church that everyone had something to share. Some had things to share which they gained through study and prayer (**psalm** and **teaching**). Others had something to share via the spiritual gifts (**revelation, another language, interpretation**). Paul's teaching isn't that congregants are simply there to sit quietly and watch the professionals do their job. Rather, his conclusion is that everything that is done in a public worship service is to be done for the building up of the group. In other words, Paul ends this extended teaching with the admonition to step out and share the good things of God with those in the church at the appropriate time.

Because spiritual gifts are not the primary purpose of church services, as an ends to themselves, we are given instruction about them. We are told that the main focus of any church service shouldn't be tongues and interpretation. These are to be allowed but in moderation because there is so much more to a service than the exercise of spiritual gifts. We are told two things:

First, **"If any person speaks in another language, there should be only two, or at the most three, each in turn, and someone must interpret. But if there is no interpreter, that person should keep silent in the church and speak to himself and to God."** An analogy I like to use regarding messages in an unknown language and interpretation is that of salt. Salt makes a great accent to a meal but too much of it actually spoils a meal. The same is true regarding the use of tongues and interpretation in a worship setting. They are not the meal but an accent designed to enhance the main dish.

Second, **"Two or three prophets should speak, and the others should evaluate. But if something has been revealed to another person sitting there, the first prophet should be silent. For you can all prophesy one by one, so that everyone may learn and everyone may be encouraged. And the prophets' spirits are under the control of the prophets, since God is not a God of disorder but of peace. As in all the churches of the saints."** Based upon what Paul has written in this extended section on spiritual gifts "prophets" refers not to an office of Prophet like those of the Old Testament but to those who prophecy in church settings. They are to be limited in the same way messages in unknown languages and interpreting of those messages are limited. They are limited for the same reason. Prophecies are not the main dish but salt to enhance the main dish.

These prophecies are not equal to the words of Prophets recorded in scripture. Nowhere in scripture are we told to stand in judgment of what scripture says. In the case of scripture the exact opposite is true - scripture stands in judgment of the reader. Here, we are instructed to judge the prophecies. No one is obligated to accept a word of prophecy simply because it is a word of prophecy. Each of us is to evaluate what is said to see if it agrees with scripture and it applies to our lives. Horrific things occur when God's people begin accepting the words of a mere human as equal to or more meaningful than the Bible itself. A great example of this is Acts 21:10-14 where Agabus gives Paul a genuine prophetic word. Paul had the obligation to stand in judgment of the prophecy and chose to move forward in his journey in spite of the word given to him.

This extended teaching ends with a section that is about spiritual gifts but somehow has been co-opted as a means of staffing the nursery with women while men dominate the pulpit. Paul writes, "**The women should be silent in the churches, for they are not permitted to speak, but should be submissive, as the law also says. And if they want to learn something, they should ask their own husbands at home, for it is disgraceful for a woman to speak in the church meeting. Did the word of God originate from you, or did it come to you only? If anyone thinks he is a prophet or spiritual, he should recognize that what I write to you is the Lord's command. But if anyone ignores this, he will be ignored.**" Let me state right off this cannot mean women are disallowed from preaching, leading in prayer, or leading in worship because of

Paul's clear teaching on the subject in 1 Corinthians 11:1-16. Obviously much more could be said on the topic of women in ministry and probably should. That is, however, the focus of a different book I am writing. Here we are dealing with the proper use and place of spiritual gifts within the church.

At issue seems to be that of the physical set up of the Corinthian church. Historians and scholars say the churches were generally set up with men on one side of the sanctuary and women on the other. In addition, they say most (not all) of the women were uneducated. They also say when a wife didn't understand something she was in the habit of speaking across the gap to her husband to ask for clarification. If this is the case, as many historians and scholars propose, you can imagine the disruption that would occur. Given that setting Paul's instruction is "*don't take the focus off what is being said and put it on yourself. Wait until you get out of church and ask for clarification.*" The principle stands true today. Nothing in a church service should be done to pull the attention away from what is taking place to have it put on us.

The final word on this topic of spiritual gifts is strong indeed. Paul writes, "**Therefore, my brothers, be eager to prophesy, and do not forbid speaking in other languages.** Paul, charged with developing healthy congregations, actually admonishes them to continue in spiritual gifts within the church. He instructs the church to be ready for the Holy Spirit to use them in spiritual gifts. He also instructs them to follow the guidelines he laid down because of their need to operate in biblical love so that everything is done (including the use of spiritual gifts) in a decent and orderly way.

In this closing chapter on spiritual gifts Paul shows the place of prophecy and tongues in the church service. He also shows the proper use of tongues in the church service and the place tongues and prophecy have within the church service. He ends, where he started in chapter 12, by sharing that spiritual gifts exist for a purpose beyond themselves.

It is true that there are wonderful Christian congregations outside of the Pentecostal/Charismatic movement which deny congregants the use of spiritual gifts. It is equally true that there are some within the Pentecostal/Charismatic movement flagrantly violating the biblical framework for a proper use of spiritual gifts. Neither group, however, simply because of their actions nullify the scriptural teaching on spiritual gifts. Rather than deny the reality of spiritual gifts each of us should actively pursue love while being ready to use spiritual gifts in a biblical way.

Section Three
The distinction between corporate spiritual gifts and
personal baptism in the Holy Spirit

Those of us who believe in and practice praying and singing in a language we have not learned during our private prayer times have been accused of many things. We are often accused of being delusional, mentally unstable, and even demon possessed. This would be bad enough if the charges came from unbelievers alone. However, the genuine tragedy of these remarks is that they are often aimed at Pentecostals/Charismatics by fellow followers of Jesus. There is a portion of God's church which actively demeans those who pray and sing in unknown languages.

Less hurtful but still tragic are those within God's family who passively accept that God does give this gift to some in the family but not it is not for them. Thankfully those in this camp far outnumber those who call God's children demon possessed simply because they pray and sing in languages they haven't learned. In this final section we will look at what is called Baptism in the Holy Spirit. This is an entirely different gift than what Paul spent 1 Corinthians 12 through 14 discussing.

Clearing Up Personal Prayer Language Beings With A Proper Perspective On Scripture.
Regarding the issue of a personal baptism in the Holy Spirit and the accompanying prayer language two key points must be clearly kept in mind. First, this has become as much an emotional issue for many people as it is an historical/biblical issue. All one need do is bring the topic up in an ecumenical setting to see how emotional it can be. Years of teaching, discussing, and debating the issue of personal baptism in the Holy Spirit

has shown me just how deeply rooted views are on the topic.

Second, regardless of a person's view on personal baptism in the 21st century it must never be forgotten that it was very much a part of the New Testament church. For this reason when we read passages pertaining to personal baptism we must do so from their perspective first.

John's Gospel As Our Starting Point
Often when dealing with the validity and availability of personal baptism in the Holy Spirit Pentecostal/Charismatic Christians begin at the wrong place. Often the starting place is Acts 1:8 or the first section of Acts chapter 2. As valuable these passages are on the subject starting from them leaves out a great deal of foundational material. For our purposes we will begin in the Gospel of John. Namely, John 16:5-15 which reads, **"But now I am going away to Him who sent Me, and not one of you asks Me, 'Where are You going?' Yet, because I have spoken these things to you, sorrow has filled your heart. Nevertheless, I am telling you the truth. It is for your benefit that I go away, because if I don't go away the Counselor will not come to you. If I go, I will send Him to you. When He comes, He will convict the world about sin, righteousness, and judgment: About sin, because they do not believe in Me; about righteousness, because I am going to the Father and you will no longer see Me; and about judgment, because the ruler of this world has been judged. "I still have many things to tell you, but you can't bear**

them now. When the Spirit of truth comes, He will guide you into all the truth. For He will not speak on His own, but He will speak whatever He hears. He will also declare to you what is to come. He will glorify Me, because He will take from what is Mine and declare it to you. Everything the Father has is Mine. This is why I told you that He takes from what is Mine and will declare it to you."

You are completely correct in noticing there is absolutely nothing mentioned about the baptism in the Holy Spirit here by Jesus. That is precisely my point. The starting point for clearly understanding the baptism in the Holy Spirit is to distinguish it from the presence of the Holy Spirit every follower of Jesus receives at salvation. This outstanding promise given to followers of Jesus is that every one of us will have the Holy Spirit following His resurrection from the dead.

There is a small group of Christians who mistakenly believe and teach that one doesn't have the presence of the Holy Spirit until he/she speaks in a language they did not learn. It seems simple enough for Jesus to have made that point here if that is what He meant. Jesus' promise to every single follower of Jesus in this passage is that we would receive the presence of the Holy Spirit as our **guide** and **counselor**.

The Apostles following up on Jesus' promise in this passage make it exceedingly clear that every follower of Jesus has the Holy Spirit. Several passages in the Epistles clearly state that a distinguishing mark of every Christian is the presence of the Holy Spirit in their lives. A small sampling of this reality includes passages such as Romans 8:8-11, Galatians 4:6, 1 Corinthians 12:13, Ephesians 4:4-6, 1 John 4:13, and 1 Thessalonians 4:8. To be clear, the Bible does not teach the distinguishing mark of a follower of Jesus is a personal prayer language he/she didn't learn. It is the presence of the Holy Spirit in their lives. The baptism of the Holy Spirit accompanied by a personal unlearned prayer language is separate from salvation itself.

Jesus begins fulfilling this outstanding promise upon his resurrection in John 20:19-23. John writes, **"In the evening of that first day of the week, the disciples were gathered together with the doors locked because of their fear of the Jews. Then Jesus came, stood among them, and said to them, "Peace to you!" Having said this, He showed them His hands and His side. So the disciples rejoiced when they saw the Lord. Jesus said to them again, "Peace to you! As the Father has sent Me, I also send you." After saying this, He breathed on them and said, "Receive the Holy Spirit. If you forgive the sins of any, they are forgiven them; if you retain the sins of any, they are retained."**

This, and not events noted in the book of Acts, is the fulfillment of Jesus' promise in John 16:5-15. The promise of salvation is not the same as a special unlearned prayer/worship language. Rather, as we see here, it is the personal presence of the Holy Spirit. Jesus does three specific things in this section to show that they are now receiving the Holy Spirit which was promised to them in John chapter 16.

First, Jesus commissions them as ambassadors for the gospel message. The single sentence, **"As the Father has sent Me, I also send you"** is the commission to carry God's message to the unsaved. It is the same in nature as the messages Jesus gives in Matthew 28:16-20 and Mark 16:14-18. Here, as the Holy Spirit in dwelled followers of Jesus they are given the vocation of living out God's kingdom and inviting others to join them in becoming followers of Jesus.

Second, Jesus breathes on them and says, **"Receive the Holy Spirit.** This is highly significant in that Jesus is showing the new life they now have as followers of the risen Savior. In Genesis 2:7 where man didn't become a living soul until God breathed life into his nostrils. In this action Jesus is giving them new life through the Holy Spirit in the same way God brought life to Adam. It is also significant for our discussion on a personal unlearned prayer/worship language. While they received eternal life spoken of in places like John 3:16 they did not receive a baptism in the Holy Spirit which included an unlearned prayer language. They received in that moment what every follower of Jesus receives because of Jesus' death and resurrection - eternal life through the presence of the Holy Spirit.

Third, they received basic instructions for how to share the reality of Jesus with others. The phrase, **"If you forgive the sins of any, they are forgiven them; if you retain the sins of any, they are retained"** has caused issue at times within the church. These problems are especially sad because they are completely unnecessary. This isn't Jesus instituting a practice of congregants confessing sins to a priest and seeking forgiveness through them. This is something much more powerful and meaningful. This is a powerful witness to the reality of a person's new life in Jesus. This English translation from the Greek text is accurate. Yet because of the differences in language we can miss the meaning if we read too quickly. The idea behind this accurate English translation from the Greek is this, "*You affirm a person is forgiven because God has forgiven them. You affirm a person isn't forgiven because God has not forgiven them.*" This is the same activity water baptism and communion offer. Just as water baptism and communion are signs to reveal those who are followers of Jesus and those who are not so we live and speak in a way that encourages fellow followers of Jesus while offering salvation to those still in their sins.

These three powerful truths are the marks of every single follower of Jesus. This isn't the domain of a professional clergy class. This isn't a means by which the masses can be manipulated or managed. When a person becomes a follower of Jesus he/she has all three events take place in his/her life.

Hopefully this short examination has shown the truth which the entire New Testament affirms. Every single follower of Jesus has the Holy Spirit. Speaking in an unlearned language in prayer or singing isn't the mark of salvation. Salvation is marked in a person because the Holy Spirit is present in his/her life.

<u>The Baptism In The Holy Spirit Is Given To Those Who Already Have The Holy Spirit.</u>

It is precisely because every believer receives the presence of the Holy Spirit at salvation that some deny the reality of a baptism in the Holy Spirit. What is most commonly offered on the subject is those experiences of people speaking in unknown languages were initial signs to the 1st century church but are no longer needed. Why they are no longer needed has never been adequately expressed but simply stated as fact. However, simply stating something to be a fact does not in fact make it a fact.

Acts 1:8 (I jokingly tell people this is the only verse in the book of Acts Pentecostal/Charismatic Christians know because we quote it so often) sets the scene for the first experience of Christians receiving the baptism in the Holy Spirit. Acts 1:8 reads, **"But you will receive power when the Holy Spirit has come on you, and you will be My witnesses in Jerusalem, in all Judea and Samaria, and to the ends of the earth."** Here we have a group of people who already have the presence of the Holy Spirit dwelling in them commanded to wait for the Holy Spirit to come on them. Personal baptism in the Holy Spirit was promised by Jesus to followers who were already saved.

Notice that Jesus' purpose for baptizing His followers (who already had the Holy Spirit in them) was not primarily so they could pray and sing in unlearned languages. Pentecostal/Charismatic Christians do a disservice to God's plans when speaking in unknown languages becomes the focus. It was not the focus for Jesus and it was not the focus for the 1st century church. The primary reason for Jesus choosing to baptize his followers in the Holy Spirit is to provide them with greater power in being witnesses. Praying and singing to God in an unknown language is a powerful blessing but it is not the primary purpose of the baptism in the Holy Spirit. The single purpose, according to Jesus, is that we may have the power to be more effective witnesses.

In Acts 2:1-4 we see the first recorded instance of those who already have the Holy Spirit in them receiving the baptism in the Holy Spirit. Acts 2:1-4 reads, **"When the day of Pentecost had arrived, they were all together in one place. Suddenly a sound like that of a violent rushing wind came from heaven, and it filled the whole house where they were staying. And tongues, like flames of fire that were divided, appeared to them and rested on each one of them. Then they were all filled with the Holy Spirit and began to speak in different languages, as the Spirit gave them ability for speech. There were Jews living in Jerusalem, devout men from every nation under heaven. When this sound occurred, a crowd came together and was confused because each one heard them speaking in his own language. And they were astounded and amazed, saying, "Look, aren't all these who are speaking Galileans? How is it that each of us can hear in our own native language? Parthians, Medes, Elamites; those who live in Mesopotamia, in Judea and Cappadocia, Pontus and Asia, Phrygia and Pamphylia, Egypt and the parts of Libya near Cyrene; visitors from Rome, both Jews and proselytes, Cretans and Arabs—we hear them speaking the magnificent acts of God in our own languages." They were all astounded and perplexed, saying to one another, "What could this**

be?" But some sneered and said, "They're full of new wine!"

Three events are connected with this first baptism experience. Two of these events only occurred here and one becomes the common pattern for those baptized in the Holy Spirit. The two one-time events are the sound of wind and tongues of fire. The ongoing common event is speaking in an unlearned language. Because this book is not a commentary time will not be spent examining each aspect of events in great length. However, a word or two about these singular events is helpful. Everyone present in our passage who received this gift of baptism was Hebrew. Everyone present in our passage was unaware of exactly what this gift of the Holy Spirit would look like. For this reason God provides them two powerful signs from the Old Testament showing them that the third part of this event (namely, speaking in unlearned languages) was genuinely from Him. Tongues of fire and the sound of wind were Old Testament signs which showed them God Himself was present and what was about to happen was from Him.

What was provided primarily for these followers of Jesus became an unintentional means for evangelism because of circumstances. With the city packed by visitors and no glass windows to keep the noise inside people began noticing what was taking place. Each of the 120 individuals were worshiping God in a prayer language they hadn't learned but the volume that day combined with the street outside being packed allowed people to hear what was being said in their native language. The primary purpose of this unlearned prayer/worship language was for those who had received it. However, on that day an outstanding side affect was that people were present to hear them glorifying God.

This event is unique in that never again in scripture does God provide the sound of wind or divided fire prior to giving the baptism in the Holy Spirit. It is also unique in that never again in scripture does this gift function as a witnessing method. It is sad that some today focus on the unique aspects of this first baptism experience with the goal of saying because they don't happen God doesn't really give His followers an unlearned prayer/worship language. In each subsequent baptism noted in the book of Acts the focus is squarely on praying in an unlearned language. The fact that the first event was unique in these ways never stopped the 1st century church from accepting the validity of praying/singing in unknown languages. They seemed to understand the reasons for this first unique experience without demanding it become the norm. A quick read through Acts 8:5-10, Acts 9:17-19, Acts 10:44-46, and Acts 19:1-7 shows that in each case it was believers (those who according to scripture already had the Holy Spirit) who were given this gift of a personal prayer language. It is the prayer language that was the norm for the 1st century church.

The Primary Purpose Of Receiving Unknown Language Is To Pray/Sing To God.
A few Pentecostal/Charismatic followers of Jesus try to meet those who don't accept unknown languages half way by combining the teachings of Paul with that of Luke in Acts. They view the baptism in the Holy Spirit as needed and available to all followers of Jesus.

However, rather than seeing the primary gift as an unlearned prayer/worship language they teach it could be any of the gifts listed by Paul in 1 Corinthians 12:4-11.

The problem with this is twofold. First, it does a great deal of harm to the scripture itself. Paul was not writing about a personal prayer language in 1 Corinthians 12-14. In chapter 14 Paul does make a few passing notes on the value of a personal prayer/worship language by the Holy Spirit. These are just passing notes, however, and not the main thrust of his writing. His main point is on spiritual gifts which operate in public worship. Luke, in writing Acts provides us with a picture of "tongues" that is completely different. Luke's focus is primarily on a follower of Jesus' personal prayer languages received at his/her baptism in the Holy Spirit. Both these authors are writing to different audiences and with different focuses. If we try to combine these two letters into the same topic, much confusion about both spiritual gifts within the church and private prayer/worship languages suffer.

Second, such a combining (1 Corinthians 12-14 and Acts) leads followers of Jesus to the misunderstanding that private prayer/worship languages are real but not necessarily available to them. In 1 Corinthians Paul is speaking about special gifts of speaking in an unknown language which is given periodically to individuals but are not permanent. Luke's focus is on a very personal private prayer/worship language that is permanent. When we confuse Paul's teaching with that of Luke many will falsely believe they are excluded from this great gift.

An oversimplification on the topic of personal baptism in the Holy Spirit with the accompanying prayer/worship language is as follows:

- Every single follower of Jesus, without exception, has the Holy Spirit in him/her (Romans 8:9-11).

- Jesus Himself gives His followers a gift of baptism in the Holy Spirit with an accompanying prayer/worship language (Acts 2:1-4; Acts 8:5-10; Acts 9:17-19; Acts 10:44-46; and Acts 19:1-7).

- Jesus' primary purpose in baptizing His followers in the Holy Spirit is to make them more effective witnesses (Acts 1:8).

Admittedly some of the issues surrounding the Holy Spirit giving people an unknown prayer/worship language today fall at the feet of Pentecostal/Charismatic Christians. Thankfully, the number of those who cause confusion is small. However this small group of well intentioned followers of Jesus have caused a great deal of confusion. There are those who try to help Jesus baptize believers in the Holy Spirit. They do this with techniques like "priming the pump" and "cleaning the temple." If you are unfamiliar with these terms you have reason to rejoice. Both these practices are unbiblical and lead to much difficulty. First, "priming the pump" is the process by which people learn to speak in an unlearned language. The difficulties with this method are numerous. Basically a well meaning Christian tells another to pick a nonexistent word and begin repeating it faster and faster until a second, third, and forth unknown word falls out of the speaker's mouth. Nowhere in scripture is this taught or even implied.

Second, "cleaning the temple" is a belief that the Holy Spirit will not baptize anyone with sin in their life. Again, this is a completely unbiblical concept. If a person must wait to be completely without sin before receiving an unlearned prayer/worship language we would all be disqualified until we got to heaven. Some go so far as to teach one must confess everything they've done wrong since accepting Jesus into their lives. Worse yet they are encouraged to tell a pastor or elder in that church. While we do each need to live in an attitude of perpetual repentance, being perfect is not a biblical requirement for receiving this gift from Jesus.

I would be remiss if a word or two about weird Pentecostal/Charismatic people was left unsaid. Over the years one of the arguments against the need for spiritual gifts or personal unlearned prayer/worship language has been the few but noticeably weird people who engage in these activities. The untrue picture that antagonists paint of all Pentecostal/Charismatic people is based on the tiny group of Christians who happen to be weird. It is true that there are some weird Pentecostal/Charismatic Christians. It is equally true that there are some weird non-Pentecostal/Charismatic Christians. The fact is that spiritual gifts and private unlearned prayer/worship languages do not make Christians weird. These individuals were weird before becoming followers of Jesus. The great news is that the presence of weird people in Jesus' family proves God will save and use all of us. Rather than seeing weird people as a reason against spiritual gifts and private unlearned prayer languages we should view this as Jesus' readiness to save and use us all.

Perhaps one of the most frustrating aspects surrounding receiving the gift of an unlearned language is the mystery we've surrounded it with. I've heard teachings on the topic of receiving this gift that lead one to believe the Holy Spirit will force the words through a speaker without any cooperation. Even our brief look at the subject in this book should make it clear that privately praying/worshiping in an unlearned language is a partnership between the Holy Spirit and the speaker. Many have actually been on the doorstep to living with this great gift without realizing it.

Have you ever been singing or praying (out loud and privately) when an unknown word slips out? When this happens most of us stop singing or praying and start again using our given language. This experience is often the Holy Spirit giving you the gift of an unlearned language. Many people open themselves to receiving the gift of the baptism in the Holy Spirit, and their unlearned prayer/worship language, simply by cooperating with the Holy Spirit in these moments. The permanent gift of an unlearned prayer/worship language is like the temporary gifts of the Holy Spirit in that they occur so effortlessly we often don't realize at first when they are happening.

If you are open to receiving your baptism in the Holy Spirit I would encourage you to continue next time that odd word or sentence comes out while praying or singing out loud to God. The Holy Spirit will provide this unlearned language as you worship and pray out loud privately.

In this section we have cleared up the issue of personal prayer languages by taking a proper perspective on scripture, saw that the baptism in the Holy Spirit is given to those who already have the Holy Spirit, and taken a brief look at the primary purpose for receiving the baptism in the Holy Spirit. The personal baptism in the Holy Spirit which includes an unlearned prayer/worship language is Jesus' gift to His followers. According to scripture, this gift expands one's ability to pray and worship privately. It also is a means, according to scripture, to build oneself up. Simply because it is separate and distinct from the gifts of the Holy Spirit doesn't mean baptism is unnecessary. It is a gift which enhances your life.

Concluding Thought

Hopefully as you've read through this short book other passages on the topic of spiritual gifts come to mind. The fact is that the 1st century church was immersed in the practice of spiritual gifts. Even the tiny book of Jude we see a note about private prayer in the unlearned language. Such a tiny book, only 25 verses, and an entire verse is devoted to praying in an unknown language. He writes in verse 20, **"But you, dear friends, as you build yourselves up in your most holy faith and pray in the Holy Spirit."** The fact that valuable space would be used for any topic - in this instance praying in an unlearned language - shows the importance of the topic addressed. The 1st century church believed in, taught, and lived with spiritual gifts and the baptism in the Holy Spirit which included a personal unlearned prayer/worship language.

Because of the enormity texts related to spiritual gifts our focus in this book has been almost exclusively on Paul's teaching in 1 Corinthians chapters 12 through 14. It is my hope that this will become a foundation to build upon as you read other texts related to our topic. This basic foundation should help each reader of the New Testament recognize sections related to spiritual gifts and see the importance they had to the 1st century church.

Secondarily, my hope as you think through the pages of this book is that you will become more gracious in your conversations. If you do not believe spiritual gifts are available to the church today, this book provides a doorway into understanding why so many of us believe what we do. For those readers who fully accept spiritual gifts as part of God's ongoing work in the world it is my hope the previous pages will provide a way of discussing the topic. For both groups it is my hope that this book shows you can disagree on a topic like spiritual gifts in the 21st century without belittling or demeaning others in God's family.

A prime example of followers of Jesus disagreeing on spiritual gifts in the 21st century takes place almost every Friday in St. Louis. A group of ministers, myself included, meet weekly at a local coffee shop for an Interdenominational Theological Discussion Group. This group of friends represents several denominations and some the non-denominational congregations. We spend half our time teasing each other and laughing together. The second half of our meeting focuses on discussing issues like spiritual gifts in the 21st century. We, like most ministers, are extremely strong willed in our opinions of scripture. However, we discuss and disagree without hurting each other's feelings or belittling each other's views. The reason for this is rooted in our love for Jesus and His church. We all agree on the key point that Jesus is the Savior of the world. We respect each other's right to worship and serve Jesus as their conscience allows.

Each of us will become far more effective in our lifestyle of witnessing to the reality of Jesus as we learn to speak graciously with those who disagree with us. My worn out joke in the Interdenominational Theological Discussion Group is "*It's ok to disagree with me. When you get to heaven God will tell you that I'm right. Until then it's ok to disagree.*" Our primary job as followers of Jesus is not to "fix" all of God's other children. It is to live and speak in such a way that the love Jesus has for the world is evident.

Those who have closed their minds to any issue within scripture have closed themselves to intellectual and spiritual growth. A great mark of spiritual maturity is the willingness to be open to what the scriptures say, especially when they disagree with our currently held beliefs. It is my hope that this book has opened your mind to the possibility of allowing the Holy Spirit to work in and through your life with both spiritual gifts and a personal unlearned prayer/worship language.